Hanukkah
In the Home
of the Redeemed

(REVISED EDITION)

The Story of the
Battle against Assimilation

ARIEL AND D'VORAH BERKOWITZ
TORAH RESOURCES INTERNATIONAL

SHORESHIM PUBLISHING, INC.
RICHMOND, MI

COVER PHOTO BY TODD BOLEN, PROFESSOR OF
OLD TESTAMENT, THE MASTER'S COLLEGE
THE BEIT HORON ASCENT ROAD
INTERNAL ARTWORK: D'VORAH VAGODA AND GARY HALZEL
COVER DESIGN AND BOOK LAYOUT: KARLOVY MEERSON
EDITING: CHARLEEDA SPRINKLE
PRINTING: WYDAWNICTWO ARKA, www.arkadruk.pl
PUBLISHED WITH A HELP OF - INSTYTUT WYDAWNICZY DRZEWO OLIWNE, POLAND

ISBN 0-9752914-9-1

SHORESHIM PUBLISHING, INC
68786 S. Main St.
Richmond, MI 48062-1545 • USA
Phone: 568-727-4300
Web site: www.shoreshim.com
E-mail: orders@shoreshim.com

PRINTED IN POLAND

DEDICATION

WE WOULD LIKE TO DEDICATE THIS BOOK TO ARIEL'S BROTHER AND SISTER

DAVID G. BERKOWITZ
AND
BARBARA A. (BERKOWITZ) TUCKER

KINDLING THE HANUKKAH LIGHTS
WAS ALWAS ONE OF THE
PRECIOUS JEWISH MIOMENTS
WE SHARED TOGETHER GROWING UP.

COVER PICTURE EXPLANATION

The picture on the cover of this booklet is a photograph of a section of highway known biblically as the Beit Horon Ascent/ Descent Road (see page 19). It is mentioned in Joshua 10:10–11 as the "road going up to Beit Horon" and the "road going down from Beit Horon."

Throughout the centuries, this road served as the main highway connecting Israel's central mountain range (including Jerusalem) with points west, such as the international coastal trading route. Modern Israel has made this road into a major highway, serving the same function. It competes with Highway 1 as the main route from Tel Aviv to Jerusalem. The Beit Horon Road also runs right behind the modern Israeli town in which these authors live!

Because of its strategic importance throughout history, many decisive battles were fought on or close to this road. Some of those battles took place in the Maccabean Wars. Judah, for example, fought Seron on this highway, chasing the remainder of the Greek-Syrians down it as the Hasmoneans scored an early victory in their war for independence.

The Beit Horon Road can serve as a visible reminder in our battle against assimilation. Historically, when Israel was faithful to the covenant God made with her, Israel was chasing her enemies down the road. But when Israel was weak, not living according to the Torah of God and attempting to become like the ungodly nations around her, her enemies were chasing Israel up the road to her very heart, Jerusalem.

CONTENTS

ACKNOWLEDGEMENTS

We would like to express our thankfulness to Karlovy Meerson as our Graphic Artist in the layout and cover design of this book. Gratitude goes to Charleeda Sprinkle for proofreading and editing the manuscript. Special thanks are also extended to Todd Bolen for his permission to use his photography, to D'vorah Vagoda for her artwork, and to Gary Halzel for the colouring pages. The authors would like to say a special thank you to DRZEWO OLIWNE Instytut Wydawniczy, a publishing company run by believers in Poland who have a special love for Israel and the Hebraic roots of their faith in Yeshua. They are handling the printing and shipping of this book.

Happy Hanukkah

We pray that during this season, the small dancing lights of the hanukkiah will help you to focus your heart upon Yeshua, the Light of the World. May a revelation of His life in us, like the Hanukkah lights, grow brighter and brighter each day. Just as we display the hanukkiah in our windows and its light reaches out into the darkness, likewise may we dedicate our lives to live out His Torah that lights our path in the darkness. We can be confident, as His covenant people, that His life in us will not be extinguished, but will constantly shine forth through us into the world.

CHAPTER 1
History and Background

CHAPTER ONE
HISTORY AND BACKGROUND

It is December. You are walking past a Jewish home. In the window, you notice an eight-branched candelabra with coloured candles lit all in a row. You hear the sound of children playing or the family singing. Then you smell the delicious aroma of fried potato pancakes coming from the kitchen. A wedding? A bar/bat mitzvah? Guess again! You have just been initiated into the joyous celebration of Hanukkah.

The Jewish people are no strangers to the art of celebration. In the book of Leviticus (chapter 23), God Himself instructs the descendants of Jacob to observe eight special *mo'adim,* מועדים (appointed times) each year to honour something that He has done for them. As one Jewish writer put it, these are "seasons of our joy."[1] In addition, outside of the Torah, the biblical book of Esther instructs the Jewish people to observe still another happy occasion commemorating one of the many incidents when He delivered the Jews from pagan oppression and persecution. This is the holiday called Purim. Then, there is Hanukkah. The Bible does not command its celebration, yet it is certainly one of the most well-known and happiest of all the Jewish holidays.

The Oppression

The Hebrew word *hanukkah* (חנוכה) means to "dedicate." It refers to a very significant historical event for Jewish people, which occurred in 165 or 164 BCE. (Both dates are used.)[2]

Alexander the Great conquered the whole Middle East, parts of Africa, and Europe in the mid to early 300s B.C.E. After he died, his vast empire was divided up geographically between his four top generals. Israel was caught in a power struggle between

---

[1] Arthur I. Waskow, *Seasons of Our Joy.*

[2] These authors prefer the 164 BCE date. Their opinion is based on convincing research done by Jonathan A. Goldstein in his translation and commentary of *1 Maccabees,* part of the *Anchor Bible Series.* See pages 273–283.

two of those generals: the Seleucid (Greek-Syrian) rulers in the north and the Ptolemaic (Greek-Egyptian) kings in the south. There was a constant seesaw of control over Israel for more than 100 years.

In the 160s B.C.E., the Greek-Syrians prevailed and ruled over Israel. Under the leadership of, perhaps, the most oppressive and cruellest of the Seleucid kings, Antiochus Epiphanies IV, Israel was subjected to an intensive Hellenization program. This was a systematic attempt to replace Jewish, biblically-oriented culture with Greek, pagan-centred, culture. In effect, if carried to its fullest, it could have eventually wiped out the Jewish people, not only through death, but also through assimilation.[3]

The core of Jewish life was the worship of the God of Abraham, Isaac, and Jacob as expressed in the Torah and manifested in the great Temple in Jerusalem. It was in these areas that Antiochus struck most heavily with anti-Jewish legislation. Among other things, he prohibited the practice of circumcision, Sabbath observance, Torah study, and Temple services. Accordingly, 1 Maccabees 1:44–50 says,

> The king sent letters by messenger to Jerusalem and the towns of Judah containing orders to follow customs foreign to the land, to put a stop to burnt offerings…to violate Sabbaths and festivals, to defile temple and holy things…to sacrifice swine and ritually unfit animals, to leave their sons uncircumcised…to forget the Torah and violate all the commandments. Whoever disobeyed the word of the king was to be put to death.

A Revolting Development

At first, to protect their lives, some Jewish people in Israel accepted Antiochus's laws, but soon a revolt broke out. Judah and his four brothers, sons of Mattathias the priest, led a courageous rebellion against Antiochus. The Jewish guerrilla army was outnumbered and out-trained compared to the Greeks. But they had one "weapon" Antiochus did not have—the God of Abraham, Isaac,

---

[3] Death was also a reality. Those who would not conform were slaughtered.

and Jacob. Judah and his family appealed to the God of their Fathers as they fearlessly led increasing numbers of Israelites to battle against the Hellenizers. They were fighting more than just a war for land. They fought for their freedom to be the people God had chosen them to be. They knew that God would be on their side and appealed to Him for their strength. For example, read one of their prayers as it is recorded in 1 Maccabees 4:30–33:

> Blessed are you, Saviour of Israel, who broke the onslaught of the mighty by the hand of your slave David, and gave the camp of the Philistines into the hands of Jonathan, the son of Saul, and his armour-bearer. Deliver this camp in the hand of your people Israel, and let them be disappointed by their infantry and cavalry. Put cowardice in their hearts and cause their bold confidence to melt, and let them totter in defeat. Make them fall by the swords of those that love You, and let all who know Your name sing hymns of praise to You.

The family which led the revolt against Antiochus was the family of the Hasmoneans. As previously stated, there were five brothers. These five sons each had rather commonly known Hebrew names. Since many others among the Israelites also held those names, it became the custom at that time to use nicknames. Thus, each of the five sons of Mattathias acquired their known nickname.[4] The names went like this:

John	. . . .	Gaddi
Simon	. . . . . .	Thassi
Judah	. . . . . .	Maccabee
Eleazar	. . . . .	Auaran
Jonathan	. . . .	Apphus

Judah became the military leader of this uprising. Since his nickname was Maccabee, his followers became known as the "Maccabees." It is unclear how this name, maccabee, originated. Some say the word "maccabee" (מכבי) is an acrostic created by combining the first letter of the Hebrew words *Mi kamocha*

---

ba'elim Adonai, מי כמוכה באלים יהוה, which means, "Who is like you among the gods?"

מכבי

Mi   מ – מי
Kamocha   כ – כמוכה
ba'elim   ב – באלים
Adonai   י – יהוה

This phrase, "Who is like you among the gods?" is a quotation from Exodus 15:11, in a context where Israel was singing praises to the Holy One for His great deliverance from the oppressive Egyptians.

A second theory says that the word "maccabee" is derived from the Hebrew word for "hammer," (*makav,* מכב) a picture of great strength. Judah, the leader was therefore called the Maccabee because of his great strength. It is interesting to note that today in Israel, there is a popular event in the Jewish world called the Maccabean Games, sporting events corresponding to the Olympics where strength and courage are stressed.

The Rededication

The Greek-Syrian oppression came to a head when Antiochus ordered pigs to be sacrificed in Jerusalem's Temple. They were to be cooked, the meat fed to the priests, and the juice poured on the altar. Spurred on by the Lord's strength and their justified anger over such detestable practices, Judah and his army secured a decisive victory over Antiochus's chief general, Lysias, in the year 164 BCE. 1 Maccabees 4:36–40 describes what followed:

> Judah said, "Now our enemies have been defeated. Let us go purify the sanctuary and restore it." And the entire army assembled, and they went up to Mount Zion. They saw the Temple laid desolate and the altar profaned and the gates burned and the courtyards overgrown with plants as "in a thicket" or like "one of the mountains" and the chambers laid in ruins. They rent their garments and made great lamentation

and put on ashes. They prostrated themselves upon the ground and sounded the signal trumpets and cried out to Heaven.

After they cleared away the debris, they made a new altar and did extensive repairs to the Temple and its courts. Then, three years to the day after Antiochus ordered the atrocities, 1 Maccabees 4:53–61 records:

> And they arose early on the twenty-fifth day of the ninth month, that is the month of Kislev, in the year 148, and they brought a sacrifice according to the Torah upon the new altar of burnt offerings which they had built. At the very time and on the very day on which the gentiles had profaned the altar, it was dedicated to the sound of singing and harps, and lyres, and cymbals. The entire population prostrated themselves and bowed and gave thanks to Heaven which had brought them victory. And they celebrated the dedication of the altar for eight days, joyfully bringing burnt offerings and sacrificing peace offerings and thank offerings...Judah and his brothers and all the entire assembly of Israel decreed that the days of the dedication of the altar should be observed at their time of year annually for eight days, beginning with the twenty-fifth of the month of Kislev with joy and gladness.

Why Eight Days?

There are several traditions as to why Hanukkah is celebrated for eight days.

1 Maccabees 4 only tells us the fact of an eight-day celebration without explaining the reason. The *Mishnah* suggests that it took eight days for the army to recapture the Temple and make a new altar, thus the eight-day celebration. (*Megilat Taanit 9*)

Without necessarily contradicting the Mishnah, the *Talmud* informs us that the Greek-Syrians desecrated all the oil purified for Temple use. Only one small undefiled jug was found with the seal still on it. It contained only enough oil to burn the Temple menorah for one day. But after the menorah was kindled, it lasted miraculously for eight days! Here is how the Talmud words it:

Our rabbis taught: On the twenty-fifth of Kislev [begin] the eight days of Hanukkah, on which lamentation for the dead and fasting are forbidden. For when the Greeks entered the Temple, they defiled all the oil in it, and when the Hasmonean dynasty prevailed over them and defeated them, they searched and found only one bottle of oil sealed by the High Priest. It contained only enough for one day's lighting. Yet a miracle was brought about with it, and they lit [with the oil] for eight days. The following year they were established as a festival, with Hallel and Thanksgiving (Shabbat 21b).

There is, yet, a third opinion. It says that Hanukkah is instituted specifically for eight days, not because of the miracle of the menorah, but because it is moulded after the holiday of Sukkot, which the Maccabees could not observe while they were still fugitives in the mountains of Judea.[5]

The weight of evidence points to this third opinion. Some background information is necessary in order to understand this explanation. First, we must know that several months lapsed between Judah's decisive victory over Lysias at Beit Zur (See Map #2) and the cleansing of the Temple. Why did Judah hesitate in cleansing and repairing the Temple for such a long period when he had the freedom to do so?

According to Goldstein, Judah hesitated because he and the godly ones with him truly expected the Holy One to perform miracles and to cause His Temple to descend from heaven. Hence, "would it not be presumptuous to restore a temple which God Himself was going to remove and replace?"[6]

Moreover, "the date at which God Himself would act against Antiochus IV, according to Daniel 7:25, was the beginning of the Sabbatical Year."[7] The sabbatical year began in the month of Tishrei (the 7th month of the Hebrew calendar). However, when

---

[5] Michael Strassfeld, *The Jewish Holidays: A Guide and Commentary*, 162.

[6] Jonathan A. Goldstein, *1 Maccabees* (The Anchor Bible): A Translation with Introduction and Commentary, 274.

[7] Ibid.

Tishrei came that year, Judah further delayed the dedication because, based on his knowledge of the Scriptures, he understood that previous dedications of the Temple were usually held during Sukkot, beginning on the 15th of Tishrei.

Knowing this, and still waiting for God's Temple to descend from heaven, Judah kept delaying the dedication of the altar for two more months. In effect, he extended the Sukkot celebration for two months![8] As time went by, Judah realized that no divine Temple would descend upon Jerusalem. Thus, he finally chose a date for the rededication and its ensuing celebration. This date, the 25th of Kislev, was chosen because it was the memorial date of the initial desecration of the Temple by Antiochus IV. The celebration lasted eight days because, in Judah's mind, this was the celebration of Sukkot for that year.

We should note that this third opinion does not mention the miracle of the oil as the reason for the eight days of Hanukkah. Indeed, while Hanukkah is one of the most historically documented of all of the Jewish festivals, none of the earliest accounts which we possess mention the miracle of the oil. This, of course, would include the story as it is recorded in 1 and 2 Maccabees, as well as the account written by Josephus—all of which were written within 200 years of the actual events.

A Divine Irony

As we have indicated, according to scholars like Jonathan Goldstein, Judah intended the dedication of the Temple to coincide with the Sukkot celebration. But, for other reasons, the observance of Sukkot that year was extended by Judah for at least two months to Kislev.

There is another piece of background information that enters into the Hanukkah picture, which makes the story even more interesting.

---

[8] Ibid.

There is a considerable amount of evidence to suggest that in the year in which Hanukkah began and the Temple was dedicated to the Lord, after having been profaned for a few years, the calendar that the Israelites were using was a defective calendar.

Israel used a lunar-based calendar, meaning that it was based on the phases of the moon. When a lunar-based calendar was used, as was the custom of several other ancient Near Eastern people in addition to the Israelites, it was periodically necessary to add an additional month into the annual calendar. In Israel, the decision to do so was fluid and was based on the proclamation of an authoritative religious body rather than being part of a fixed annual calendar. During the years of the Antiochian persecution, this religious body was prohibited, as was the celebration of the annual holy days. Thus, before the dedication of the Temple, no adjustments (intercalations) were made to the Jewish calendar.

Consequently, in the year of the dedication, 164 BCE, Tishrei fell in the middle of summer, rather than in the autumn, when it usually occurs. That means that the celebration of Sukkot was in the summer rather than in the fall, such as in October. Furthermore, Kislev that year came in the autumn. To be specific, the celebration of Hanukkah began on 25 Kislev, which was 16 October 164 BCE in the properly adjusted calendar, according to Goldstein.[9]

There is a certain irony in this date. If the Israelites were using the properly adjusted calendar, 25 Kislev would actually have fallen on or close to the actual 1st day of Sukkot! Jewish people today, based on calculations made during the Second Temple Period following the Maccabean revolt, use such an adjusted calendar. That is why 25 Kislev now occurs during the

---

[9] Goldstein, *1 Maccabees*, 165 and 283. We have attempted to simplify a rather extensive series of evidence and reasoning that Jonathan Goldstein presents in his commentary on 1 Maccabees. The arguments and evidence are powerful and convincing. We strongly encourage the reader to consult Goldstein's commentary, specifically pages 273–284.

western month of December (sometimes late November)—well after the season of Sukkot, which falls roughly during October. The irony for the Maccabees is that they fully intended to celebrate the dedication as a Sukkot festival. Fully anticipating a miraculous intervention by God, they waited for God to send His Temple from the heavens, and therefore they kept on delaying their observance of Sukkot. When they finally realized no such miracle was going to take place, they scheduled their rededication of the Temple. However, the date they chose actually fell during Sukkot on the properly adjusted Jewish calendar.[10] Whether or not they realized this, it was God's sovereignly ordained timing for the dedication of the Temple in that day.

We hope this was not too confusing for some. Whenever one discusses calendar matters and dates in relation to ancient events, particularly events with the Jewish people, there are always a multitude of factors to consider. That is why it is never helpful or accurate to dogmatically enforce any given date from antiquity unless there is ample and irrefutable evidence for it.

---

[10] This date is according to Goldstein's calculations based on his research.

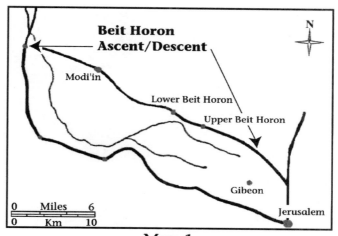

Map 1
The Beit Horon Ascent/Descent

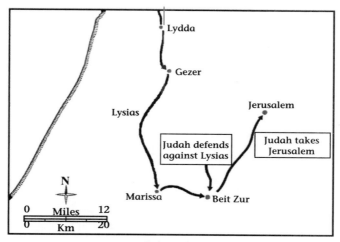

Map 2
Judah's Victory over Lysias
and location of Beit Zur

CHAPTER 2
Assimilation

CHAPTER TWO
ASSIMILATION

Who Were the Real Enemies?

Some historians suggest that the Greek-Syrians, though they were certainly the Judeans' foreign enemy, were not Israel's greatest enemy. Instead,

> These scholars maintain that the villains of the story are Jewish Hellenizers – namely, a group of Jewish aristocrats who wished to form a Greek polis or city-state...When segments of the people opposed these Hellenizers, they called upon their powerful supporter, Antiochus, to back them up with Syrian troops.[11]

Hence, according to this view, the Israelites' real enemies were fellow Jews who sought assimilation in the form of Hellenization. Indeed, assimilation has always been the number one enemy of the people of Israel! Indeed, the testimony of 1 Maccabees bears this out:

> At that time, lawless men arose in Israel and seduced many with their plea, "come, let us make a covenant with the gentiles around us, because ever since we have kept ourselves separated from them we have suffered many evils." The plea got so favourable a reception that some of the people took it upon themselves to apply to the king, who granted them the liberty to follow the practices of the gentiles. Thereupon they built a gymnasium in Jerusalem according to the customs of the gentiles[12] and underwent operations to disguise their circumcision, rebelling against the sacred covenant. They joined themselves to the gentiles and became willing slaves to evil doing (1 Maccabees 1:11–15).

---

[11] Strassfeld, *The Jewish Holidays*, 165.

[12] "In a Greek gymnasium all the physical exercises and sports were performed in complete nudity." Goldstein, *1 Maccabees*, 200.

The Nature of Assimilation

What is assimilation? The verb "to assimilate" means "to become like the people of a nation, or other group in customs, viewpoint, character or other attributes."[13] In other words, assimilation is what happens when a person or people group become like the people around them. During the historical time period in which Hanukkah took place, the people of Israel began to become like the Hellenists. The core issue was this: Would the Torah (God's Covenant) be honoured or would the people succumb to pagan pressures and think like, act like, talk like, and look like the pagan Hellenists?

What would motivate one to assimilate into another people or culture? As we answer this question, we must realize that there are some forms of assimilation, which are not altogether detrimental. It could be helpful and good for a person or people to assimilate into a people or culture that is guided by biblical principles. Certain elements and levels of a healthy assimilation are desirable for new immigrants to a country or for someone entering a people group with a God-given task to work among that people.

However, on the other hand, others levels of assimilation can have seriously detrimental effects on a person or on a people group. This is especially true for the ancient (and modern!) Israelites. What motivated them to assimilate? The answer is simply summed up in one word: survival. They were not immigrating to another nation with the hopes of becoming integrated into that new host nation. Rather, they were being unwillingly oppressed by a foreign people and subsequently forced to adopt into the invader's culture upon pain of death for refusal to do so. If the entire population gave in to those pressures, the result would have been a massive dismissal of a Torah witness. If the people would not give in, the result could have been the destruction of the race. What were they to do?

---

[13] *The World Book Dictionary* © World Book, Inc.

Survival

Some would say that survival is the most important objective for a people group. That might be true in some cases. But preserving and living the Word of God, a higher objective, was at stake. Yeshua understood this issue correctly and taught about it this way:

> Anyone who loves his father or mother more than Me is not worthy of Me; anyone who loves his son or daughter more than Me is not worthy of Me; and anyone who does not take his cross and follow Me is not worthy of Me. Whoever finds his life will lose it, and whoever loses his life for My sake will find it. (Matthew 10:37–39)

According to this passage, our Messiah taught that there are some cases in which one would sacrifice his own life for the sake of being faithful to our covenant relationship with God. This is the thrust of the words, "…and whoever loses his life for My sake will find it."

The Scriptures taught this same truth to the ancient Israelites, both by precept and example. The precept is taught in passages like Deuteronomy 30:19–20, which states:

> This day I call heaven and earth as witnesses against you that I have set before you life and death, blessings and curses. Now choose life, so that you and your children may live and that you may love the Lord your God, listen to His voice, and hold fast to Him. For the Lord is your life, and He will give you many years in the land He swore to give to your fathers, Abraham, Isaac and Jacob.

Here, the Torah says that real life—both physical and spiritual—is lived through a covenantal relationship with the Holy One. Anything other than commitment to faithfulness to this covenant relationship with Him and His Word is walking in the realm of death. To choose a life apart from God and His Word is already living in death. Therefore, if one is given the choice to assimilate or to follow God's Word, the choice is obvious. To walk outside the covenant relationship is walking down the path that is death anyway. Thus, it is better to be faithful to our covenants with God and to physically lose our life for choosing to do so, than to choose to be unfaithful to God and to gain physical life for a season.

The book of Daniel reports one of the greatest biblical examples of this principle. The story begins in Daniel 3:1: "King Nebuchadnezzar made an image of gold, ninety feet high and nine feet wide, and set it up on the plain of Dura in the province of Babylon." Then, in Daniel 3:4–6 the king had it proclaimed:

> This is what you are commanded to do, O peoples, nations and men of every language: As soon as you hear the sound of the horn, flute, zither, lyre, harp, pipes and all kinds of music, you must fall down and worship the image of gold that King Nebuchadnezzar has set up. Whoever does not fall down and worship will immediately be thrown into a blazing furnace.

However, it was soon reported to the king:

> But there are some Jews whom you have set over the affairs of the province of Babylon—Shadrach, Meshach and ,Abednego—who pay no attention to you, O king. They neither serve your gods nor worship the image of gold you have set up. (Daniel 3:12)

The Jewish offenders were arrested and brought before the powerful King Nebuchadnezzar. The king threatened these three faithful ones with death in the fiery furnace if they did not worship the image. But

> Shadrach, Meshach and Abednego replied to the king, "O Nebuchadnezzar, we do not need to defend ourselves before you in this matter. If we are thrown into the blazing furnace, the God we serve is able to save us from it, and He will rescue us from your hand, O king. But even if He does not, we want you to know, O king, that we will not serve your gods or worship the image of gold you have set up." (Daniel 3:16–18).

The story continues by recounting how they were cruelly and mercilessly thrown into the fire. But then an amazing event occurred. The king noticed that not only did the fire not harm the men, but also that he could see "four men walking around in the fire, unbound and unharmed, and the fourth looks like a son of the gods" (Daniel 3:25). God delivered them. He honoured their faithfulness.

Rather than assimilate into the pagan Babylonian culture and worship their gods, the three men chose to honour their God. As a result, this proved to be a powerful and effective testimony to King Nebuchadnezzar. He was never the same after that. We read in Daniel 3:28–29:

> Then Nebuchadnezzar said, "Praise be to the God of Shadrach, Meshach and Abednego, who has sent His angel and rescued His servants! They trusted in Him and defied the king's command and were willing to give up their lives rather than serve or worship any god except their own God. Therefore I decree that the people of any nation or language who say anything against the God of Shadrach, Meshach and Abednego be cut into pieces and their houses be turned into piles of rubble, for no other god can save in this way."

To be sure, faithfulness to withstand assimilation into a pagan culture does not always have this kind of ending! But the message the Scriptures intend to tell us through life accounts like this one is that it is our calling to remain abiding with God no matter what our circumstances may be. Those who do so will remain within the place of life, whether in this life or the next. Moreover, in every instance in which we resist the temptation to assimilate, we will always encourage others who desire to do the same.

The Maccabean Boys

These principles were at stake during the days of the historical events of what became the first Hanukkah. It is true that there were an increasing number of Judeans that were more willing to abandon the Torah than to die for it. But there was also a faithful remnant of true believers in the God of their fathers who were faithful to His Covenant.

Mattathias and his five sons were the most well-known examples. Jerusalem was already desecrated by Antiochus's order for swine to be sacrificed upon the altar of the Temple. Many of the well-to-do of the city were succumbing to the pressures to Hellenize. But this faithful priest of Modi'in (located about 20 miles to the north and west of Jerusalem on the Beit Horon Ascent/Descent) risked his life to resist the assimilating efforts of Antiochus's emissaries in Modi'in. When told to worship an idol in the town centre, someone went forward to bow down to it. As he did, the faithful priest Mattathias stepped out and boldly slew him for idolatry. He and his five sons then headed for the foothills that surround Modi'in and took refuge from the revengeful onslaught of Antiochus's soldiers.

While living in the hills, the Maccabean brothers, under the capable leadership of Judah, began the guerrilla war against the Greek-Syrians. More and more were attracted to their cause. Eventually, Judah led a force up the ancient Beit Horon ascent road, the ancient approach to Jerusalem, with the intention of retaking Jerusalem, the capital. On the way there, the Holy One gave him an outstanding victory over a sizeable trained Greek-Syrian army, paving the way for a successful campaign for Jerusalem. The rest is the story of Hanukkah.

A Perpetual Problem

The temptation to assimilate has always been one of the most dangerous threats to the Jewish people. Ever since we left Egypt, we have always been inclined to worship the gods of the people who surrounded us and, consequently, to adapt the ungodly lifestyles that accompanied such a decision. This problem continues to remain a serious issue for Israel even today.

For example, after centuries of severe persecution from Christianized Europeans, the Jewish people of Germany felt they finally had a chance to survive and succeed while they were living among the German people; however, not without a cost. All they thought that they had to do was to make sure that their main identity was that they were Germans and not Jews. To do that meant that the Jewish people of pre-World War II Germany became one of the most assimilated Jewish communities in the world. This is a historical fact.[14] They apparently thought that abandoning Torah and Jewish traditions would provide security for them. They were tragically mistaken. The treacherous arms of the Holocaust embraced all—the religious, the godly, and the secularly assimilated alike.

God and Assimilation

What does God have to say about assimilation? We have hinted at the answer to this before. Let us now be more explicit.

God says in the Torah, "Be holy for I am holy." He repeated this statement to teach the Israelites that they were not to be like the Canaanites who lived in our midst within the Promised Land. Why? The answer is that the Canaanite religion and its corresponding lifestyle were among the most corrupt of the entire ancient world. That is an historical fact. Israel, as the chosen and redeemed people of God were to have nothing to do with that pagan idolatrous life. Israel, instead, was called to be separate and to function as a light shining forth the glory of the nature of the true God.

In addition to the calls for holiness from the Holy One Himself, it is essential to note that Israel was a people who were made holy by the election and call of God. It was the Holy One who redeemed them from Egypt. As freed slaves, they were to think and live as ex-slaves, never to go back to "Egypt" again under the "yoke of bondage."

The history of the Hebrews enslaved in Egypt can function as what we refer to as a "Torah picture." A Torah picture is a teaching picture. When the Israelites lived in Egypt, being subjected to horrible servitude, they became an effective illustration of what it means for all of us to live under the bondage and influence of the "kingdom of the snake." This was the intention of the Holy One

---

[14] See p. 6 of *History of the Holocaust: A Handbook and Dictionary* by Abraham J. and Hershel Edelheit.

for purposes that would benefit all mankind in all ages of human history.

For example, just as Israel was enslaved to serve a kingdom utterly opposed to the God of Israel, so are all who are born in this world. We were all born enslaved to sin (Romans 6:11–14). In addition, just as the Egyptians opposed the God of Israel, so also does the "god" of this world stand in defiance against the Holy One. Moreover, when Israel was enslaved by Egypt, life was hopelessly miserable with no end in sight. It was the same with all of us. Under "Egypt," our lives were controlled by the powers of the snake and sin. We were not able to deliver ourselves.

Indeed, there were many similarities between our lives outside of Messiah and the lives of the Israelites as slaves in Egypt. Our redemption as proclaimed in the Good News was and is accurately pictured by the redemption of the Hebrews from slavery in Egypt. The Israelites were not able to redeem themselves. Neither were we able to do so. Like the ancient Israelites, we were not able to set ourselves free from bondage to sin and Satan. Furthermore, the Torah indicates that it took the mighty and merciful arm of God to set Israel free from their slavery. God redeemed us from slavery to sin in exactly the same manner. Our redemption was accomplished through the shed blood of *the* Passover lamb, Yeshua the Messiah, through His death and resurrection on our behalf and in our place.

The question for us who are redeemed is How much of our past slavery in "Egypt" do we still permit to be an influence in our thinking and, therefore, in our lives? Remember, for our purposes at this point, we are using the word "Egypt" in a figurative sense. We believe that God's intention in the Scriptures was to use Egypt as an illustration of the kingdom of sin and death, or the kingdom of Satan. "Egypt" is that kingdom out of which God calls His Son (and all those sons which are in Him). "Egypt" holds God's children in the bondage of slavery, a bondage that constricts God's people from knowing and walking in their true biblical spiritual identity as children of God.

When we were slaves in Egypt, we allowed the *voice* of Egypt to shape our lives and to form our identity as slaves. That identity is what we believed to be our true selves until the Word of God intervened in our lives. The Word of God then stood up to the *voice* of Egypt in our lives and told us the truth. Therefore, as new creations in Messiah, we know that the Scriptures teach us that it is no longer necessary to live under the burden of all that was our identity in Egypt.

How much are we giving in to a process of assimilation in our lives as redeemed people? Centuries ago, it was the Torah that stood up to Egypt and said "No! God's people will not let themselves live under conformity to you. God's people will worship the one true God and serve Him alone!"

It is the same today. Torah continues to oppose "Egypt" and continues to tell the truth! It is the truth that truly sets people free to be who they were created to be! The problem of assimilation is resolved when God's people rise up against "Egypt" and, with God's Word, say, "No! We will not let ourselves live under conformity to you. We will worship the one true God and serve Him alone!" This is who we are! The life of one who worships the one true God is defined by the covenant, which the God of Israel has given to us. That covenant document is His Torah. That covenant document is the Scriptures from beginning to end.

There Is an Answer

Romans 12:1–2 provides the answer to the temptations of ungodly assimilation. The weakness that succumbs to temptation comes from our flesh. We define the "flesh" as "the mind patterned after this world."

In short, to whom are we listening? If we let ourselves be governed by the flesh, then we will give in to ungodly assimilation. But, Romans 12:1–2 says,

> Therefore, I urge you, brothers, in view of God's mercy, to offer your bodies as living sacrifices, holy and pleasing to God—this is your spiritual act of worship. *Do not conform any longer to the*

pattern of this world, but be transformed by the renewing of your mind. Then you will be able to test and approve what God's will is—His good, pleasing and perfect will. (Italics ours).

In this passage, the Greek phrase translated "do not be conformed" are the words *mei suscheimatízesthe,* μη συσχηματιζεσθε. The word, *suscheimatízesthe* means to be conformed to or shaped by something. Grammatically, this is a present negative imperative. That means that God is saying, "stop continually being conformed to, shaped by, or living after the pattern of this world."

How does one "listen to" this verse? The text says, "but be transformed by the renewing of your mind." In order to not be conformed any longer (assimilated) to this world, our minds must be renewed. Thus, we see that the problem is with our thinking more than anything else. It is our thinking that must be guarded. Therefore, the Scriptures teach us, "We demolish arguments and every pretension that sets itself up against the knowledge of God, and we take captive every thought to make it obedient to Messiah" (2 Corinthians 10:4–5).

Our passage in Romans even tells us how to take our thoughts captive, that is, how to renew our minds. It says that we are to be "transformed" by the renewing of our minds.

The word "transformed" (*metamorfoústhe,* μεταμορφουσθε) means a transformation or change that can be both outward and inward. Moreover, this word, "transformed," is in the passive mood, which means that we cannot transform ourselves. It is something done to us. How can this be? It is simple. We let the Word of God wash our minds and renew our thinking. We let the Scriptures tell us what to think and how to think. We stop letting ourselves be continually influenced by the thinking patterns of "Egypt" and give our minds over to what God says in His Torah.

The Newer Covenant Scriptures tell us that *every* new creation person in Yeshua has the mind of Messiah. This one simple statement has many ramifications if we think it through carefully. First, we realize that since Yeshua is the Word made flesh and dwelling among us (John 1:1–14), then Yeshua in us is the Living Word. Next, we realize that the Living Word and the Written Word is the same Word. Furthermore, we read in James chapter 1 that the Written Word is also our "mirror." It is through this "mirror" that we can come to know our new creation self. That is one of the many reasons why we need to immerse ourselves continually in the Scriptures. For it is through reading the Word of God that we can come to know the mind of Messiah, which we now have as new creations in Messiah.

The Word of God, then, is our mirror through which we will really be able to see the ways in which we have been assimilated and how far from our true identity we are living when we walk in our flesh.

Remember our working definition of assimilation is "to become like the people of a nation, or other group in customs, viewpoint, character or other attributes." Biblically, assimilation is identified as "being conformed to, shaped by, or living after the pattern of this world." When we assimilate in a detrimental way, what has happened is that the "pattern of the world" became our "mirror."

Now, our goal is to learn to use the Word of God as our mirror in order to be "transformed" from the image of self we learned while living in "Egypt." When we know the Word of God to be our mirror, we learn how to see truly, and then we are free to learn how to live consistently with who we now are as new creation people in Messiah Yeshua.

In writing this Hanukkah manual, it is our hope that each reader will take the time to ponder deeply the depth of these truths. In reality, all of these truths are part of the Good News of the finished work of Yeshua. If we really "hear" what the Good News is proclaiming to us, we will finally be living in "the place of hearing."

The "mirror" – James 1:22–25

The First Hanukkah

The word *Hanukkah* is a term taken from the Torah. It is found in Numbers 7:84. This section speaks of the dedication of the Tabernacle (*Mishkan*) by Moses. The text says, "This was the dedication of the altar, ‏זאת חנוכת מזבח‎." The word "dedication" is the Hebrew term, hanukkah.

It is significant that this word, hanukkah, is first used in the context of the dedication of God's house, God's Tabernacle. In a real sense, therefore, this momentous event in the life of the children of Israel was the first Hanukkah. They dedicated this place where the presence of God resided in ancient Israel.

In God's plan, eventually, the Tabernacle gave way to the Temple, built by King Solomon in Jerusalem. Because of Israelite unfaithfulness, the first Temple was destroyed by the Babylonians in 586 BCE. Around 515 BCE, after the Babylonian exile was over, some of the Israelites upon their return to the Land of Israel under the leadership of Zerubbabel, began to build the Second Temple. This is the Temple that was desecrated in 165 BCE by Antiochus Ephphanes IV, the Hellenist and the enemy of the Maccabeans.

The Second Temple was completely and luxuriously remodelled by Herod the Great in the first century BCE. This remodelling was finally completed in the seventh decade of the Common Era, only to be utterly destroyed soon thereafter by the Romans in 70 CE.

God, however, prepared His people to function without a temple. He did so through prophecy and instruction. The prophecy came from the Messiah Himself and is found in Matthew 24:1–2. Here we read:

> Yeshua left the Temple and was walking away when His disciples came up to Him to call His attention to its buildings. "Do you see all these things?" He asked. "I tell you the truth, not one stone here will be left on another; every one will be thrown down."

This was graphically fulfilled about 40 years later when the Romans completely totalled the building.

The instruction came through Sha'ul (Paul) of Tarsus. There are a few places where he told his students that we, the body of Messiah, are the temple of the Spirit of God. For example, we read in 1 Corinthians 3:16–17,

> Don't you know that you yourselves are God's temple and that God's Spirit lives in you? If anyone destroys God's temple, God will destroy him; for God's temple is sacred, and you are that temple.

and again in 1 Corinthians 6:19:

> Do you not know that your body is a temple of the Spirit of God, who is in you, whom you have received from God?

The Greek word behind the English "temple" in these passages is *naos* (ναος). This term is used frequently in the Septuagint to translate the Hebrew word *hekhal,* היכל. The Hekhal was not the temple area in general. Rather, it referred specifically to the actual Temple building. This is, therefore, how Paul was using hekhal's Greek equivalent, noas. He was saying that the body of believers is the actual temple building of the Spirit of God.

> Paul stands quite clearly on the basis of Jewish tradition when he speaks of the naos: the redeemed community is the temple of God (1 Corinthians 3:16f), and God's Spirit dwells in her (1 Corinthians 6:19; c.f. 1 Kings. 8:16f. where God's name dwells in the temple.)[15]

There is one more thought to share from 1 Corinthians 3: 16–17 and 6:19. In both cases, the Greek pronoun translated "you," is in the plural. This emphasizes even stronger that we, as the collective body of Messiah, are God's holy temple.

Because of this biblical connection, the festival of Hanukkah is a most appropriate time to renew that awareness of dedication to the Holy One by asking Him for the power to enable us to be victorious over any assimilation that might be attempting to engulf us.

---

[15] Colin Brown, gen. ed., *The New International Dictionary of New Testament Theology*, vol. 3, p. 784.

CHAPTER 3
The Changing Face
of Hanukkah

THE CHANGING FACE OF HANUKKAH

Although Hanukkah has been celebrated for many centuries, it was not until recent times that the holiday began to gain the importance it enjoys today among the Jewish people. However, we do know that Hanukkah was celebrated during the time of Yeshua. John 10:22–30 records a time when Yeshua was in Jerusalem at the Temple teaching during the "Feast of Dedication," one of the more ancient names for Hanukkah.

There is a possible historical reason why Hanukkah was not emphasized for many centuries. In traditional Judaism, if the Talmud teaches something, it becomes important for Jewish people. Although the Talmud mentions Hanukkah, it does so in a very sketchy manner. In fact, it mentions only briefly the great Hasmonean military victory and focuses mainly on the supposed miracle of the oil. However, in the earliest celebrations of Hanukkah, the opposite was the focus.

The reason for this historical shift on the emphasis of Hanukkah may be explained like this:

> The Hasmonean [another name for the Maccabean family] dynasty, with the passage of time, became Hellenized and, more important, some of them opposed and even persecuted the rabbis. This dark later history superseded the bright period of their beginning.[16]

In addition, the rabbis understood the Torah's teaching that Israel's king should only come from Judah. But the Hasmoneans were Levites. Yet,

> the Maccabees had made themselves and their offspring kings, after expelling the Syrian-Greek empire. In itself, that was a violation of the ancient Israelite custom, which requires the priests and the king to come from different tribes.[17]

---

[16] Strassfeld, *Jewish Holidays*, 163.

[17] Waskow, *Seasons of Our Joy*, 91.

This usurpation of the Israelite throne was an anathema to the Torah-conscious rabbis. Since the Talmud is the product of the rabbis, they did not want to emphasize the fact that a great military victory was led by a family who later became their enemy.

Hence, it has become rather evident that the rabbis of the Talmudic period, desiring to de-emphasize the Hasmonean victories, may have invented the legend of the miracle of the oil. This legend, then, could become, for their purposes, the focal point of celebration instead of the Maccabean military victory. Because the Talmudic rabbis exert much influence in all of Jewish society, their viewpoint of the purposes of Hanukkah has, therefore, permeated the entire Jewish people since the writing of the Talmud.

In the late Second Temple period, when Yeshua celebrated Hanukkah, it was a time when the people of Israel remembered the great military victory that God granted the Maccabeans and how the Holy One enabled them to rededicate the Temple for services rendered unto God. It was not, therefore, until a few centuries later that the celebration of Hanukkah shifted from being strictly a military victory celebration to a commemoration of the miracle of the multiplication of oil.

The Remembrance of Heroes

By the time of the Middle Ages, as Hanukkah continued to change and develop, "the focus of Hanukkah remained on the miracle of the oil, though stories of bravery of the Maccabees were well-known."[18]

Among these stories, mostly found in 1 and 2 Maccabees, was the tale of Eleazar. He was a scribe in his 90s who refused to eat pork and then subsequently died of torture inflicted by his enemies while attempting to force him to do so. Even more familiar is the story of Hannah and her sons. Hannah watched

---

[18] Strassfeld, *Jewish Holidays*, 164.

each of her seven sons die a horrible death rather than eat pork or worship an idol. Finally after hearing all of them confess their faith in the true God, she herself was put to death for the same reason.

These and other stories of martyrdom served to provide much encouragement for the Jewish people who were under much persecution during the Middle Ages. They continue to do so even to this very day.

Another addition to the Hanukkah celebrations during the Middle Ages was the reading of a scroll called *Megilat Antiochus*. This is a scroll containing the story of Hanukkah patterned after some of the other *megilot*, particularly *Megilat Esther*.[19] *Megilat Antiochus* was the story of Hanukkah, emphasizing the military victory, as well as the miracle of the oil. Furthermore, *Megilat Antiochus*, originally written in Aramaic, is the earliest rabbinic work on Hanukkah.

> It is a very important document because the story of the miracle of oil appears in it for the first time. The accounts of this miracle in the Talmud are based on this scroll...It is the first rabbinic interpretation of Hanukkah. Scholars have pointed to the purity of its Aramaic style as evidence of its antiquity...The scroll, therefore, must have been written in the period between 70 and 100 C.E. There is ample evidence to corroborate this conclusion.[20]

We can find this story in many *siddurim* (weekday Jewish prayer books) today, particularly the *siddur* edited by Rabbi Philip Birnbaum.

---

[19] A *megilah* is a scroll. Through the centuries, the rabbinic sages have singled out five special biblical books to be read on certain special holy days in the Jewish calendar year. These five books were written on scrolls by themselves for convenience when reading. The list is as follows: On Purim, *Esther* is read. On Passover, *Song of Songs* (*Song of Solomon*) is read. On Shavuot, *Ruth* is read. On Tisha B'Av (late July to early August), *Lamentations* is read in connection with the remembrance of the destruction of both the First and Second Temples. Finally, *Ecclesiastes* is read during Sukkot.

[20] Abraham P. Bloch, *The Biblical and Historical Background of the Jewish Holy Days*, 94–97.

Hanukkah Today

Today Hanukkah has become a major festival of celebration for Jewish people the world over, especially in Israel, where among other things, it means a week off from school for the children! It is a Jewish national holiday where the victory of a small army over a larger force is emphasized. At the same time, we also remember the legend of the miracle of the oil by lighting our Hanukkah lights for eight nights. This celebration is, of course, enhanced by joyous songs and the savoury tastes of delightful foods cooked in oil.

In Israel, we know Hanukkah is coming a month ahead because of the sudden appearance of *sufganiyot* in the shops along the streets and in the market places. What are sufganiyot? They were (until very recent years) Israel's only doughnut. Sufganiyot are jelly-filled raised doughnuts, sometimes dusted with powered sugar, found fresh and hot out of the oven all over Israel for only this season and its celebration. (We provide you with a recipe to make them for yourselves. See Appendix A.)

In America and in much of the Diaspora, Hanukkah is also a time of gift-giving. This custom might have developed because of the influence of Christmas in the lands of the Diaspora. Whatever the origin of this, it does serve to add to the joyfulness of the holiday.

Moreover, it has for centuries been the Eastern European Jewish custom to give special Hanukkah *gelt* (money) to the children to help make their Hanukkah more fun. Today, it is traditional to use chocolate gelt—coin-shaped chocolate, wrapped in silver or gold foil to look like a silver or gold coin.

A Messianic Celebration

Hanukkah is also a Messianic celebration. There are several ways in which the celebration of Hanukkah focuses on the Messiah.

First, when we think of Israel's salvation from foreign oppression, we are reminded of that deliverance in the future, spoken of by the prophets, when Messiah Himself will rescue His people from all oppression. This is one of the richest sources of hope for the persecuted people of God.

The prophet Zechariah speaks of a time in the future when the enemies of Israel will advance toward Jerusalem. In Zechariah 14, we are told that just when things seem like all is about to be lost, God Himself will descend upon the Mount of Olives in Jerusalem and defeat Israel's enemies. He will then remain in Jerusalem and set up His glorious Kingdom of righteousness, teaching Torah from His throne in Jerusalem. When the Messiah sets up His glorious kingdom, He will not only come to Israel's defense, but He will also rescue all of His chosen ones from every trouble and distress.

Secondly, the authors of this little booklet would like to suggest an important facet of Hanukkah for us to consider worthy of our attention and remembrance in this time of festive celebration. It is another way in which the celebration of Hanukkah can center on the Messiah. We can focus on Him who defends those who choose to live a life dedicated to righteousness and faithfulness to His covenants, instead of succumbing to the assimilating forces of their generation.

That which the Maccabees deeply understood and lived is also aptly expressed in the teaching of Romans 12:1–2:

> Therefore, I urge you, brothers, in view of God's mercy, to offer your bodies as living sacrifices, holy and pleasing to God—this is your spiritual act of worship. Do not conform any longer to the pattern of this world, but be transformed by the renewing of your mind.

The Maccabees acutely understood the influences of the Hellenization process. They had no intention of accepting a culture, which at its roots, intended to wipe out all semblances of a biblically-based lifestyle and theology. The nation of Israel was called to exist at the crossroads of civilization as a light to the nations. Their total existence was a profound commitment not to be "conformed to the pattern of this world."

Accordingly, we read in Exodus 11:7 that the Lord distinguishes between "Egypt" and Israel. As previously stated, one reason why God raised up Egypt was to be a Torah picture of the kingdom of darkness. And one reason He raised up Israel was that Israel could function as the Torah picture of all of God's children who are called out of the kingdom of darkness because they are the children of Light. We, as believers in Yeshua— whether physically part of Israel or "grafted" into Israel—are the assembly of "the called-out ones." We were called out from among the nations to be the remnant of true worshippers of the one true God. In so doing, we are the bearers of the Light of the Kingdom of Light. The Living Torah, Yeshua, and the written Torah are the Light of that Kingdom.

Our celebration of Hanukkah will reach its fullest when we focus on these truths. Beginning with remembering the historical account of the Maccabean victory over assimilation, we can call to mind all of the other times in our history when our people remembered who they were as the children of God and chose to courageously stand up for that calling. Remembering those critical moments in our history will encourage us in our generation to live out our calling as the called-out ones God intended us to be and to resist the forces of assimilation in our day.

The message of Hanukkah will also remind us to use the weapon which combats assimilation—the Word of God. There is an eternal weapon that in every generation stands up against the godlessness, lawlessness, and corruption of man. It is the Torah of our God, lived through the lives of His redeemed. We are instructed to live out God's Word just like the Maccabeans of old who dedicated themselves to offer the true sacrifices unto God in the Temple. We, too, are taught to present our bodies as living sacrifices unto God, which is our spiritual service of worship. Hence, let us with unswerving devotion embrace the instructions of Romans 12:2, choosing not to conform any longer to the pattern of this world but being transformed by the renewing of our minds.

There is an eternal weapon that in every generation stands up against the godlessness, lawlessness, and corruption of man. It is the Torah of our God lived through the lives of His redeemed.

CHAPTER 4
Traditional Celebration

CHAPTER FOUR
TRADITIONAL CELEBRATION

In this section, we will share some traditional and not-so-traditional ways to celebrate Hanukkah, especially for believers in Yeshua. It is important to remember at this point that Hanukkah is a happy event, full of spiritual meaning for everyone. Like the rest of the celebrations of life, this festival also requires careful preparation in order to benefit the most from it.

A word of explanation is necessary at this point. Hanukkah is distinctly a Jewish festival. For the most part, Christian folk have either chosen to ignore it or have simply never known about it. However, the fact that Hanukkah is a Jewish celebration does not mean that all believers in Yeshua cannot enjoy it. On the contrary, the Scriptures indicate that non-Jewish believers in Yeshua are grafted in to Israel (Romans 11) and, therefore, have become a meaningful part of the people of Israel (Ephesians 2). One of the implications of being part of the people of Israel is the freedom to share in Israel's joys and sorrows, especially as they are expressed in Israel's holy days. Hanukkah is a special time where the people of Israel celebrate the great victory God gave them over those who attempted to destroy them, both from within and without. This is certainly a celebration in which all of God's people can participate.

We are presenting next in this Hanukkah manual a traditional Jewish way of celebrating Hanukkah. After all, this is probably the only way that Hanukkah has been celebrated throughout the centuries! In Jewish theology the word "tradition" sometimes refers to the "unwritten laws and doctrines, or any one of them, believed to have been received by Moses from God and handed down orally from generation to generation."[21]

---

[21] *The World Book Dictionary* © World Book, Inc.

Similarly, in some Christian theologies, the term "tradition" speaks of "the unwritten precepts and doctrines, or any one of them, held to have been received from Jesus and his apostles and handed down orally since then."[22]

Indeed, in those Jewish religious circles, many religious laws have been developed over time, designed to govern religious Jewish people in their observance of Hanukkah.

However, since Hanukkah is not a biblically commanded event, we do not see a biblical imperative to be governed by such religious laws. Consequently, when we use the word "tradition," we are not using it in a strict Jewish religious sense. Rather, we are using the term "tradition" to refer to "the [simple] handing down of beliefs, opinions, customs, and stories, such as from parents to children, especially by word of mouth or by practice."[23] Hence, we mean "long-standing customs."

Having said that, however, we must recognize that most of the Jewish traditions are designed to enhance one's celebration of Hanukkah. They can help to make our celebration easier and more meaningful. Therefore, we are presenting a rather traditional Jewish way of celebrating because, based on our experience, it will augment our celebration of Hanukkah. This is providing, of course, that one is not limited by a rigid set of man-made religious laws, but guided by the sensitivities of the Spirit of God.

The Implements

1. A Jewish Calendar

Hanukkah lasts for eight days and begins on the 25th day of the Jewish month of Kislev. This can be anywhere from late November or any part of December in our Western calendars. One may locate the day on which the 25th of Kislev falls in a particular year by searching Jewish Web sites on the Internet. Or,

---

[22] *The World Book Dictionary*, op. cit.

[23] Ibid.

one may simply purchase a Jewish calendar at the local Jewish book store through a local synagogue or Jewish Community Centre, through the Internet, or at a book and card shop. Better, yet, just ask a Jewish neighbour! (One may also consult Appendix A in this booklet.)

2. A Hanukkiah
The second implement that is needed to celebrate Hanukkah is an eight-branched candelabra. This is called by two names in Hebrew: a *hanukkiah* or a *hanukkah menorah*. Either name is acceptable. Actually there should be room for nine candles, but this will be explained later.

This hanukkiah can be purchased at any Jewish book or gift shop. However, one does not need to limit one's creative abilities! A hanukkiah can be made in any way, as long as there are places for nine lights. The older, more traditional ones, are usually made from brass or silver. Some of the modern ones are made from almost any materials, such as wood or glass. Please look in chapter six under the heading of "Crafts" for a few ideas about how to make your own hanukkiah.

3. Candles
Next, we come to the lights themselves. There are basically two choices about the kinds of lights on the hanukkiot: wax candles or olive oil with wicks. Whatever method one chooses, there must be enough light to last for eight days. (Yes, we know there are electric hanukkiot, but we "purists" prefer not to use them!) If candles are chosen, then care should be taken to match the size with the hanukkiah. There must also be a supply of candles to last for eight days. This is approximately 45 candles. They can usually be purchased in a box with the number already counted out.

4. This guide or a Siddur (Jewish Prayer Book)
You will be saying some wonderful blessings before you light your lights. The traditional blessings are found here in this Hanukkah manual or written in most weekday *Siddurim* (Jewish prayer books).

The Procedure

Remember that the first day of Hanukkah is on the 25th day of Kislev. In a Jewish calendar system, the day begins the night before. Thus, the first Hanukkah light is lit after sundown the evening before. For example, if the 1st day of Hanukkah is on Tuesday, the 8th of December, then the first Hanukkah light is lit Monday the 7th of December in the evening after sundown.

1. The Lighting

The lights are placed in the hanukkiah from right to left as you are looking at the front of the hanukkiah. On the first night, one candle is lit; the second night, two are lit, and so on. However, the candles are lit starting left to right! The idea is that you are lighting each day's new candle first.

The first candle to be lit is called the *shammas* or "servant" candle. This is the ninth candle on your hanukkiah. It is usually in a separate position, so you can know which one it is. With this candle, all of the other regular candles are lit. After lighting all of the candles for that night, place the shammas back into its position, still lit.

Light the candles *after* the blessings are made. If there are children in the family, perhaps they could take turns lighting the candles with the watchful guidance of the parents.

2. The Blessings

All major (and some seemingly minor) events in a Jewish person's life are preceded by a blessing or two. This speaks for itself. Making a blessing over what seems like a simple, mundane act, transforms that act into a holy activity, acknowledging the presence of God at its very core. On Hanukkah, there are three traditional blessings, which are said before one lights the candles. All three are said the first night; the first two are traditionally pronounced on all subsequent nights. Here are the traditional blessings:

Note: In the transliteration, we have distinguished between the Hebrew letters *khaf* (כ) and *chet* (ח) by using a kh for a khaf and a ch for chet. To English speakers, particularly, please do not pronounce the ch in chet (ח) as a ch in Charles. Rather, it is a guttural sound, like the Scottish ch in lach.

Blessing #1

ברוך אתה יהוה אלוהינו מלך העולם אשר קידשנו
במצוותיו וציוונו להדליק נר של חנוכה. אמן

"Barukh atah Adonai Elohenu Melekh ha'olam asher kid-shanu b'mitzvotav v'tzivanu lehadlik ner shel chanukkah." Amen

"Blessed are You Lord our God, King of the universe, Who has sanctified us with His commandments and has commanded us to kindle the Hanukkah light." Amen.

(**Note**: It is true that God did not "command" us to light Hanukkah lights. However, He did command us to praise and to worship Him. If done properly, this is a tremendous act of worship and praise. So in that light, this blessing can be said. Or, one may simply paraphrase or change the blessing by substituting the word "permitted" for the word "command." In that light, we offer this untraditional, but appropriate, alternative blessing:)

ברוך אתה יהוה אלוהינו מלך העולם אשר קידשנו
במצוותיו והבטיח לנו להדליק נר של חנוכה. אמן

"Barukh atah Adonai Elohenu Melekh ha'olam asher kid-shanu b'mitzvotav vehivtiach lanu lehadlik ner shel chanukkah." Amen

"Blessed are You Lord our God, King of the universe, Who has sanctified us with His commandments and has permitted us to kindle the Hanukkah light." Amen.

Blessing #2

ברוך אתה יהוה אלוהינו מלך העולם שעשה ניסים
לאבותינו בימים ההם בזמן הזה. אמן

"Barukh atah Adonai Elohenu Melekh ha'olam she'asah nissim l'avotenu b'yamim hahem b'zman hazeh." Amen.

"Blessed are You Lord our God, King of the universe, Who has wrought miracles for our forefathers in those days at this season." Amen.

Blessing #3

ברוך אתה יהוה אלוהינו מלך העולם שהחייינו
וקייימנו והיגיענו לזמן הזה. אמן

"Barukh attah Adonai Elohenu Melekh ha'olam shehechiyanu, v'kiyemanu, v'hegianu, lazman hazeh." Amen.

"Blessed are You Lord our God, King of the Universe, Who has kept us alive, sustained us, and brought us to this season." Amen.

3. Music

After the blessings are said and the candles are lit, a traditional Jewish hymn called *Maoz Tzur* (מעוז צור) is sung. The theme of this hymn is the strength of God and His role as Israel's deliverer—the main theme of Hanukkah. You can find the words and music at the end of this guide. Later, we will also provide some additional songs to be used each night in your family candle -lighting time.

4. Food

Following the formal celemony of the candle-lighting, the party begins! An integral component of the festivity is, of course, food—as always on every happy occasion! However, on Hanukkah, it is traditional to eat foods cooked in oil. Oil is one of the symbols of this festival because the large menorah of the Temple was illuminated by the use of olive oil. This menorah lit in full view is the symbol of this festival of dedication.

In many places, potato pancakes called "latkes" are eaten. Of course these are fried in oil. As we have already noted, in Israel, jelly-filled and oil-fried sufganiyot (doughnuts) are eaten. In the end of this guide, we will also provide some tasty hanukkah recipes.

5. Games

Another part of the fun is when we play Hanukkah games. Please refer to the section entitled "Games" for a description of some time-honoured Hanukkah games.

CHAPTER 5
"Eight Days of Enlightenment" A Hanukkah Daily Study Guide

CHAPTER FIVE

"EIGHT DAYS OF ENLIGHTENMENT" A HANUKKAH DAILY STUDY GUIDE

In the remaining part of this booklet, we are offering an original Hanukkah daily devotional guide for the family or group. Such a devotional guide is never used in the traditional celebration of Hanukkah. However, since these authors know that this holiday can be a tremendous personal and family time of worship and learning, we offer this devotional guide in the hopes of the blessing that it can be during these specially set apart eight nights.

This guide is designed for use assuming one is a believer in Yeshua. It is traditional in that in many Jewish circles, a series of Scriptural readings is shared for each of the separate nights of Hanukkah. This list is as follows:

First Night
Genesis 1:1–5, 14–18

Second Night
Isaiah 5:20–24

Third Night
1. Psalms 115:5–6
2. Job 24:13, 17; Job 18:5–6
3. Jeremiah 25:10
4. Ezekiel 32:8

Fourth Night
Isaiah 42:5–7, 16; 45:7; 42:16

Fifth Night
1. Daniel 9:17
2. Psalms 43:3; 36:10; 18:29; 56:14
3. Proverbs 20:27
4. Job 33:29–30

Sixth Night
1. Psalms 27:1; 104:1–2; 119:105; 19:9
2. Proverbs 6:23

Seventh Night
1. Proverbs 4:18
2. Psalms 97:11–12
3. Isaiah 2:5; 9:1; 60:1
4. Exodus 10:23

Eighth Night
1. Isaiah 30:26
2. Zachariah 14:6–7
3. Isaiah 60:19–20

If you like, you can use this list of Scripture passages in your readings during each day. Then, each night after lighting the candles in the usual traditional manner with the blessings, spend time as a family talking together and learning about the Holy One, using the daily guide we provide next in this Hanukkah manual. Note: If you decide to sing the suggested songs for each night, prepare music sheets in advance.

Otherwise be prepared with music, which you would like to use on these special evenings.

Day One

This Time and This Season

Theme:
"This Time and This Season" (Words taken from one of the blessings.)

Read:
Read the story of Hanukkah in 1 Maccabees. Read especially Chapter four. The story can also be read from one of many children's books about Hanukkah. In addition, it would be good to read *Megilat Antiochus* from the *Siddur* (Prayer Book).

Ask Questions:
Ask some key questions just to be sure that all have understood the story:

1. What problems did the Israelites face? From whom?

2. Who were some of the Israelite heroes?

3. Why were they heroes?

Discuss:
It is important that we remember what God has done for us in the past because, in doing so, we remember God! Discuss this concept together.

Read:
Read Psalm 145:1–7.

Prayer:
Thank God for bringing us safely to this time and this season and for blessing us along the way.

Sing:
"Melech Ozer" and "Maoz Tsur"

Notes, Comments, and Memories

Day Two

He That Keeps Israel

Theme:
"He That Keeps Israel"

Do:
Briefly recount the historical events leading up to the first Hanukkah. (These can be gleaned from chapter one of this booklet).

Read:
1. Read 1 Maccabees 4:30–59—The story of the historical event.

2. Psalm 4:2–3—God's comments on the nature of the Maccabean plight.

3. Psalm 18:1–3, 28–40—The source of the Maccabees' victory.

Discuss:
Talk about how the above passages from the Psalms shed light on what was happening in the lives of the Maccabees. Discuss how the Maccabees lived out their knowledge that "the Lord has set apart the godly for Himself" (Psalm 4:3).

Ask Questions:
With the historical context in the forefront of everyone's minds, ask the following questions:

1. Why do you think it is good, especially for those of us who are in Yeshua, to celebrate Hanukkah?

2. What can Hanukkah teach us about God? About His grace? About His promises?

Point out that God made promises to keep Israel from perishing as a people and that no one can utterly destroy Israel. God has promised to always keep a remnant of Jewish people as a faithful witness to Him.

Furthermore, God has made promises to always keep those who are His own.

3. What does all of this have to teach us about the keeping power of God?

Look up the following passage to further underscore God's keeping power: John 10:22–30 and Romans 8:31–39.

Prayer:
Thank God for saving us by His grace and for keeping us eternally with Him.

Read:
Isaiah 42:5–9—Read this while everyone is still quietly finishing their prayers and just before singing.

Sing:
"He That Keepeth Israel" and/or "David, Melech Yisrael"

Notes, Comments, and Memories

_____

_____

_____

_____

_____

_____

Day Three

Israel That Keeps unto God

Theme:
"Israel That Keeps unto God"

Discuss:
Use pages 12–14 of this manual to read to your family and guests the two excerpts from I Maccabees 4. Then discuss the following ideas:

1. After they cleared away the debris, they made a new altar and did extensive repairs to the Temple and its courts. Talk about the actions involved in the rededicating of something to God. Then, discuss the actions that may be involved in the rededicating of our lives to God.

2. Talk about the Hebrew word *"hanukkah."* It means "dedication."

3. The title for this holiday is derived from Numbers 7: 84, which recounts the dedication of the tabernacle in the time of Moses. In Hebrew it reads, *"zot hanukkat hamizbeah,* זאת חנוכת המזבח, which means, "This was the dedication of the altar..."

Ask Questions:
1. What are some of today's idols in which we could be entangled?

2. Can objects as well as people be dedicated to God? Explain.

3. Go over Psalm 95:6–7 and Romans 12:1–2. How do these two passages work together to picture the true meaning of our lives?

Prayer:
Talk to God about our desire to be dedicated to living the life to which He has called us. Ask Him to open our eyes to the subtle and the not-so-subtle forces of assimilation that may be trying to lure us away from that calling. Pray for our own resolve as a

family that we be dedicated to preserving and living the Word of God in today's ungodly society.

Read:
Psalm 89:13–18

Sing:
"Come into the Holy of Holies"

Notes, Comments, and Memories

_____

_____

_____

_____

_____

_____

_____

Day Four

He Has Done Great Things

Theme:
"The Great Things God Has Done"

Discuss:
What was the real miracle at Hanukkah? To understand what we mean by this question requires a more lengthy explanation. We will do our best to be as concise as possible.

There is good historical evidence that the miracle of burning oil for the eight days of Hanukkah never happened! The story says that when the Jewish people wanted to light the great Menorah in the newly dedicated Temple during the Maccabean revolt, there was only enough oil to last for one day. But God did a miracle. He caused the oil to last eight days, long enough to purify more oil.

The problem with this story is that none of the most ancient sources for the actual history of Hanukkah (1 and 2 Maccabees and Josephus) mentions the above miracle. This means that the earliest and best sources for the history of Hanukkah never mention this commonly believed event of the miracle of the oil. Actually, the miracle is first mentioned in an early rabbinic work called *Megilat Antiochus*, which, in turn was used for the basis of the teaching about it in the Talmud (compiled about 650 years after the first Hanukkah).

In short, what some historians believe is that the ancient rabbinic sages, spiritual descendants of the Pharisees, did not want to emphasize the great victories of the Maccabean family (their real family name was the Hasmoneans). The reason for this is believed to have stemmed from the fact that the Hasmoneans were descendants of the Levites. They were priests. Yet, following their victory, not only did they assume the spiritual head of Israel (rightly so), but they also took over the political leadership of Israel, a position believed to be reserved only for the descents of Judah. Furthermore, during their political reign, they persecuted the Pharisees.

Given this historical backdrop, it is easy to see why the spiritual descendants of the Pharisees, the Talmudic sages, would not want to emphasize the great spiritual and military victories of the Hasmoneans. Accordingly, they stressed the legend about the miracle of the oil, as if to place the emphasis on God's role in the story. However, as we have already indicated, the best historical sources seem to indicate that this miracle never happened. It is not as if God was incapable of doing such a miracle. He was/is, of course. But that is not the point. Choosing to be true to history is sufficient in honouring the God who performs miracles in the preserving of His own children. We do not need to be supportive of legends. Our God is a God who has demonstrated Himself in human history. It is to this God and to His mighty deeds that we give praise in these special eight days of celebration.

Having said that this miracle of the light probably never happened does not mean that there was no miracle at Hanukkah. Indeed, there were great miracles! There were both spiritual and a military miracles. Perhaps the greatest miracle was that in the increasingly assimilated and Hellenistic Jewish society, there rose up a family of faithful Torah-observant, God-fearing Jews who made a courageous stand against those who were ignoring the Covenant of God. But not only did Mattathias encourage his own family to live for the God of Israel, he also, in turn, was able to inspire others in his nation to do so. In the end, God honoured that courage and dedication to Him and to His Covenant with His people.

The second miracle came on the battlefield. The Maccabees and their followers were vastly outnumbered. Although they were equipped and trained, their Antiochian enemies were more so. Yet, through courage, and faith in their God, the Lord granted them the miraculous military victories they needed.

What about the eight days? Hanukkah was celebrated for eight days. Because the Maccabees hid in the hills and bravely fought the enemy through their guerrilla warfare, they were not able to celebrate Sukkot. Therefore, when they celebrated their victory in Jerusalem they included in their celebrations the eight-day celebration of Sukkot.

Back to our initial question: What was the real miracle at Hanukkah? The answer is that God granted both a spiritual and a military victory to those who were dedicated to Him.

1. As we celebrate Hanukkah, what similar miracles can we remember?

2. What other great works of preservation has the Lord done for which we can sing praises to His Name?

3. Discuss the great things God did for the Maccabees.

4. Why did God do these great things for the Maccabees?

After a time of discussion, ask someone to read this excerpt from the commentary in our booklet:

The Maccabees acutely understood the influences of the Hellenization process. They had no intention of accepting a culture, which at its roots, intended to wipe out all semblance of a biblically based life-style and theology. The nation of Israel was called to exist at the crossroads of civilization as a light to the nations. Their total existence was to be a people who would not conform to "the pattern of this world." Accordingly, we read in Exodus 11:7 that the Lord distinguishes between "Egypt" and Israel. One reason why God raised up Egypt was to be a Torah picture (a teaching picture) of the kingdom of darkness. And one reason He raised up Israel was that Israel could function as the Torah picture of all of God's children who are called out of the kingdom of darkness because they are the children of Light. We, as believers in Yeshua, whether physically part of Israel or "grafted" into Israel, together we are the assembly of "the called-out ones." We were called out from among the nations to be the remnant of the true worshippers of the One true God. And, in so doing, we are the bearers of the light of the Kingdom of Light. The Living Torah, Yeshua, and the written Torah are the Light of that Kingdom.

Our celebration of Hanukkah will reach its fullest when we focus on these truths. Beginning with remembering the historical account of the Maccabean victory over assimilation, we can call to mind all of the other times in our history when our people remembered who they were as the children of God and chose to courageously stand up for that calling. Remembering those critical moments in our history will encourage us in our generation to be the called-out ones God intended us to be and to resist the forces of assimilation in our day.

Ask Questions:
1. Can we expect God to do whatever is necessary to help us when we choose to serve Him, even in the face of great danger? Explain.

2. Relate the times in your life when this has happened for you.

3. What purposes was God accomplishing when He did those things for the Maccabees? For us? For you?

Prayer:
Praise God and thank Him for He has done great and mighty things throughout all of history!

Read:
Malachi 2:4–7, 4:4; Zachariah 8:20–23

Sing:
"Great and Wonderful"

Note:
For a more in-depth Bible study related to this theme, study John 10:22–31 and Yeshua's remarks concerning Hanukkah:

1. What feast is in reference here? (v. 22)

2. Where was Yeshua teaching? (Solomon's Colonnade, part of the Temple area)

3. What did the people want to know? (v. 24)

4. What proofs did Yeshua give them? (v. 25)

5. Why do you think Yeshua cites His miracles in this context? (Remember Hanukkah and miracles!?)

6. Why couldn't some believe in Him? (v. 26)

7. What happens to His sheep? (verses 27–29—Note the emphasis on the keeping power of God.)

Notes, Comments, and Memories

_____

_____

_____

_____

_____

_____

Day Five

Bond-Servants of Yeshua

Theme:
What it means for us to be bond-servants of Yeshua

Discuss:
Single out the Shamash light, the servant light you used to light the rest of the on the hanukkiah. Use it as an object lesson. Point out that the Shamash can picture the Messiah.

This special candle is used to give its light to the other candles. In this regard, read John 1:9. Furthermore, in the end, the Shamash is given a place of its own, a separate place, a place of honour. See Philippians 2:1–11.

Ask Questions:
1. What does this candle do?

2. What is it called? Why?

3. Why do you think it is placed separate from all the rest of the candles?

4. In how many ways did Messiah serve us? Use the following Scriptures to help you in your answer. Can you think of more passages?

John 17:1–8 with Psalm 19:7–11—He served us by delivering God's words to us.

Read:
Isaiah 52:13–53:12

1. How does Yeshua serve as an example for us to be true servants of our Father in Heaven?

2. In which ways are we called to serve Him?

Isaiah 41:8–10, Isaiah 49:3

Look again at Philippians 2:1–11

Galatians 5:13–14

Prayer:
Ask God to help us to yield ourselves to righteousness and to continue to serve the Lord by serving one another in love.

Sing:
"Humble Thyself in the Sight of the Lord" and "Let Us Exalt His Name Together"

Notes, Comments, and Memories

_____

_____

_____

_____

_____

_____

_____

_____

Day Six

So Others Can See and Know

Theme:
Sharing the message with others

Discuss:
It is traditional for Jewish people to place their hanukkiot in a window so that others may see and know that their home is a Jewish home. For those of you who are not Jewish, placing your hanukkiah in the window is a significant way to stand together side by side with the Jewish people. Let us not forget that, as believers in Yeshua, we have been grafted into Israel. As believers who understand the importance of commemorating the fact that God is a God who goes before His people in battle, we too can put our hanukkiah in the windows of our homes. We are His "called-out ones," called to stand out as lights in a dark world. We are the living stones of His Temple dedicated to His service.

We can stand courageous and strong against the ever-present powers of assimilation that endlessly seek to get us to put a "bushel over our light." We stand up to these "armies" and say, "We are the people of the Living God!" We know as Joshua knew, "No one will be able to stand up against you all the days of your life" (Joshua 1:5). No matter what the army facing us looks like, we will not back down from what we are called to be—the "called-out ones" of the Living God, to Him be the glory and power for ever and ever. Amen!

Questions:
1. Why is it important for people to know that we are dedicated to being lights in a dark and evil world?

2. What bearing does Matthew 5:14–16 and Acts 1:8 have on this whole discussion?

Pray:
Pray for at least one person you know who does not yet know Yeshua. Pray for those in the Land of Israel. Pray for us here in the Land that we can be lights for the Messiah in our communities. Pray that we all as believers in Yeshua the Messiah will embrace the Torah for what it truly is, Yeshua Ha Torah—Yeshua living in us! Yeshua said, "If anyone believes in Me, out of his innermost being will flow streams of living water." Pray that we will let His life flow from us here within the land of Israel! Pray that we will again "see the distinctions between the righteous and the wicked, between those who serve God and those who do not" (Malachi 3:18).

Read:
Isaiah 9:2

Sing:
We recommend that you purchase ahead of time the Avraham Fried CD which contains the song, "Don't Hide From Me." On this night play that song. Visit the local Jewish bookstore or surf the Internet for the CD. The CD is produced by a company called Noam. The code for the CD is Noam, CDH566

Notes, Comments, and Memories

_____

_____

_____

_____

_____

_____

_____

Day Seven

With Gladness and Joy

Theme:
Why we celebrate with great gladness and joy

Discuss:
Review the story again. Emphasize the gladness and joy the people had when God granted them victory over their enemies and permitted them to rededicate the Temple. Reread 1 Maccabees 4:59 where it says "all the congregation of Israel decreed that the days of the rededication of the altar should be observed this season...with gladness and joy."

Read:
1 Peter 2:4–5, 9
Romans 12:1–2

Ask Questions:
1. What does it mean for our lives to be "a living sacrifice"?

2. Of what does our spiritual service of dedication/ worship to God consist? Make sure you answered this question using the very wording of the Scriptures themselves.

3. What is the real source of our joy? John 17:13 (Read the whole of John 17 and talk together about this passage. Then turn together to Isaiah 58 and read verses 13 and 14.

4. Now discuss this passage in light of John 17.

Prayer:
Pray by using expressions of joy, praise, adoration, and thanksgiving to the Lord for the joy we have in Messiah Yeshua.

Read:
Psalm 149:1–4

Sing:
"Then Shall the Virgin Rejoice",
"Trees of the Field" and
"Roni, Roni"

Sing other joyful biblical songs and try some family dancing!

Notes, Comments, and Memories

_____

_____

_____

_____

_____

_____

_____

_____

Day Eight

The Light of the World

Theme:
Learning how Hanukkah can picture Yeshua as the Light of the World

Discuss:
What have we learned these past eight days? Talk about applying the things we have learned to our lives. To enhance the discussion, you might want to review the importance that the menorah played in the ancient Temple in Jerusalem. Why did the Lord first instruct the Israelites to place a menorah in the Tabernacle? What symbolism would it have carried?

Read:
John 1:1–14; 8:12; 9:5

Ask Questions:
1. What does this passage call Yeshua?

2. What does verse 9 mean when it says Yeshua gives light to everyone?

3. With all the candles lit, what is one thing we have plenty of? (Light!!)

4. What are some things light does for us?

5. What happens to darkness in the presence of light?

6. In what ways, therefore, does Yeshua function as the Light of the World?

Read:
Psalm 36:7–10

Pray:
Turn out all household lights. Have everyone gaze at the hanukkiah lights while someone reads Isaiah 60:1–5. Pray for the Lord to bring us to know ourselves to be the shining lights

in Yeshua that we are in Him. Pray that together we will come to know the depth of the truth: "In Your light, we see light" (Psalm 36:9).

Sing:
You might want to conclude this year's Hanukkah celebration by singing "Hatikva," the Israeli National Anthem. Look in chapter six under the heading "Songs" for the words of "Hatikva."

Notes, Comments, and Memories

_____

_____

_____

_____

_____

_____

_____

CHAPTER 6
Games, Food, Songs, and Crafts

CHAPTER SIX

GAMES, FOOD, SONGS, AND CRAFTS

Games

1. Dreidel

The most famous Hanukkah game is called "*dreidel*." "Dreidel" is a Yiddish word for "top." It is a four-sided top with Hebrew letters on each side of it. Such tops can be purchased at Jewish community centres, Jewish bookstores, on a visit to Israel, or through the Internet. In addition, one may always make his/her own dreidel. It is a top of any size that spins well and has four sides on which certain Hebrew letters are written. There is no limit to one's creativity in designing the dreidel!

The four letters are the first letters in four Hebrew words which mean "A great miracle happened there" (*Nes Gadol Haya Sham,* נס גדול היה שם). Perhaps if we list the letters, as we do below, it will all be easier to understand:

Nes gadol haya sham.

"A great miracle happened there."

Nes, miracle: Nun (נ)
Gadol, great: Gimmel (ג)
Haya, happened: Heh (ה)
Sham, there: Shin (ש)

Thus, the four Hebrew letters on the four-sided dreidel are: נ - ג - ה - ש.

There is a variation on the dreidels in Israel. First, they are usually referred to by their Hebrew name, *sevivon*, סביבון/ Second, the Hebrew letters are slightly different. When we live outside of Israel, we say that a great miracle happened *there*, meaning *in Israel*. However, for those who live in Israel, that is rather inapproproiate! Since they live in the Land where the story of Hanukkah took place, they say, "A great miracle happened *here.*" Thus, the Hebrew letters on the dreidel are the same except for the final letter. Instead of a *shin* (ש) standing for the word, "there," we place a *peh* (פ), standing for the word, "here." Accordingly, the letters on an Israeli dreidel are: נ - ג - ה - פ.

It is helpful to understand why this game is played on Hanukkah before we provide the simple instructions.

The game called dreidel began sometime in the Middle Ages in Europe. During that time, Jewish people often faced severe persecution from people who called themselves Christians. The Jewish people were often prohibited from celebrating their holy days and festivals. Hanukkah was an especially sensitve time because the holiday celebrates Jewish nationalism.

However, these prohibitions did not deter a very resourceful people! It may have been illegal to celebrate religious and Jewish national days, but it was not illegal to play games. Thus, from a simple children's game, the Jewish people developed a way to carry on the message of Hanukkah, so that even children would understand and remember. The prinicple message of Hanukkah was simply placed on the four sides of a simple top. When Hanukkah arrived, the top was spun and the message of Hanukkah was remembered by the the four Hebrew letters written on the top, the dreidel.

Now for the instructions:

1. As many players that desire may play the game. Sometimes, if there are many who want to play, several dreidel groups can be formed.

2. The group must decide what they are playing for, that is, the victor's prize. This prize can be any number of inexpensive things such as peanuts, beans, little pieces of chocolate, or pennies. Special candy has been developed called Hanukkah *gelt.* The Yiddish word "gelt" means "gold" or money. Hanukkah gelt is simply chocolate coins wrapped in gold or silver foil. You can purchase them in almost any grocery market or candy store. Once

the group decides upon the prize, each player contributes his/her share to the common pot. This pot is the prize.

3. Play begins when one player spins the top. (The group needs to decide who can go first.) When the top finishes spinning, it lands with one of the four Hebrew letters showing. The Hebrew letter that shows determines the next move. A good way to learn what happens is:

Nun (נ) — gets nothing (of the pot)
Gimmel (ג) — gets all (of the pot)
Heh (ה) — gets half (of the pot)
Shin (ש) — puts something in (the pot)
Peh (פ) — puts in (the pot)

4. Play ends when the players decide it is over. This usually happens when folks get tired of playing. At the conclusion of the game, the winner is the person who has the most of the prize.

Have Fun!

2. Mattathias and Antiochus Issue Orders
This game is much like the game "Simon Says." Here, the leader issues orders to the participants standing in a row. He commands them "kneel before me," "follow me," "at ease," etc. Each order is prefaced with either Mattathias says" or "Antiochus says." If the order is given by Mattathias it is to be obeyed. If given by Antiochus, it is to be ignored. Whoever fails to respond correctly is eliminated from the game.

3. Put the Shamash on the Hanukkiah
Prepare a huge hanukkiah drawn on cardboard and hang it on the wall. Each player is given a candle made from construction paper and a straight pin. One at a time, blindfold the players, spin them around, and allow them to try to pin the candle on the shamash holder. The candle closest to the shamash-holder is the winner.

4. Hidden Dreidel
Have one player leave the room. While he is gone hide the dreidel. Then the player re-enters the room and searches for

the hidden dreidel. The other players sing a Hanukkah song, singing louder as the searcher comes close to the hidden dreidel and softer as he moves away.

Hanukkah Music

Various audiotapes or CDs and music books can be purchased at Jewish bookstores, through mail order, and from the Internet. Some of the most popular songs and music, such as "Maoz Tzur," are included in the helpful Hanukkah book called, *Treasures of Chanukkah,* listed in the bibliography. Here are some of the more popular titles that you should look for:

Hanukkah, Oh Hanukkah
Mi Y'maleil? (Who Can Retell?)
My Dreidel
Hatikvah
Ma'oz Tzur

Hatikvah התקוה

Background
The words to Israel's national anthem were written in 1886 by Naphtali Herz Imber, an English poet originally from Bohemia. The melody was written by Samuel Cohen, an immigrant from Moldavia. Cohen actually based the melody on a musical theme found in Bedrich Smetana's "Moldau."

English Translation
As long as the Jewish spirit is yearning deep in the heart, with eyes turned toward the East, looking toward Zion, Then our hope — the two-thousand-year-old hope — will not be lost: To be a free people in our land, the land of Zion and Jerusalem.

Hebrew and Transliteration
Kol ode balevav P'nimah   כל עוד בלבב פנימה

Nefesh Yehudi homiyah   נפש יהודי הומיה

Ulfa'atey mizrach kadimah   ולפאתי מזרח קדימה

Ayin l'tzion tzofiyah.	עין לציון צופיה
Ode lo avdah tikvatenu	עוד לא אבדה תקותנו
Hatikvah bat shnot alpayim	התקוה נת שנות אלפים
L'hiyot am chofshi b'artzenu	להיות עם חפשי בארצנו
Eretz Tzion v'Yerushalayim.	ארץ ציון וירושלים

Maoz Tzur מעוז צור

Background
The words of this song are from approximately the 13th century CE. Tradition says that it is written by a man named Mordecai. One reason for this tradition is that his name is encrypted in the first letters of the five stanzas. The music comes from somewhere between the 15th and the 18th centuries. There are many verses, but the first stanza is usually the one that is sung by most.

English Translation
O God, my saving stronghold, to praise You is a delight! Restore my house of prayer, where I will offer You thanks. When You will prepare havoc for the foe who maligns us, I will gratify myself with a song at the altar.

Hebrew and Transliteration

Ma'oz Tzur Yeshuati	מעוז צור ישועתי
Lkhah n'eh Lishabe'akh	לך נאה לשבח
Tikkun beit Tefilati	תכון בית תפלתי
V'sham todah nizabe'akh	ושם תודה נזבח
L'et tkhin matbeakh	לעת תכין מטבח
Mitzar hamnabe'akh	מצר המנבח
Az egmor b'shir mizmor	אז אגמור בשיר מזמור
Khanukat hamizbe'akh (2x)	חנכת המזבח

Mi Y'maleil? (Who Can Retell?)

This version of this popular Hanukkah song is not the most literal translation, but it is a very popular rendition.

English Translation
Who can retell the things that befell us?
Who can count them?
In every age a hero or sage came to our aid.

Listen! In days of old in Israel's ancient Land
Maccabee led the faithful band.
Now all Israel must as one arise
Redeem itself through deed and sacrifice.

Hebrew Transliteration
Mi yimalel g'vurot Yisrael Otan mi yimneh?
Hein b'khol dor yakum hagibor, go-el ha-am.

Sh'ma! Ba-yamim ha-heim ba-z'man hazeh
Maccabee moshiya u'fodeh

U'v'yameinu kol am Yisrael
Yitacheid yakum l'higa-el.

Mi ye-ma-lel g'vu-rot Yis-ra-el? O - tan mi yim - neh?
Who can re-tell the things that be-fell us? Who can count them?

Hen be-khol dor ya - kum ha-gi-bor go - el ha - am,
In ev-'ry age, a he - ro or sage came to our aid!

Sh'ma! Ba - ya - mim ha - hem ba-z'man ha - zeh,
Hark! In days of yore, in Is-rael's an - cient land, Brave

Ma - ka - bi mo - shi - a u - fo - deh,
Mac - ca - be - us led the faith - ful band. But

u - v'ya - me - nu kol am Yis - ra - el,
now all Is - rael must as one a - rise, Re-

yit - a - hed ya - kum le - hi - ga - el.
deem it - self thru deed and sac - ri - fice.

*This may be sung as a round. Second voice starts at [II] from the beginning.

Chanukkah, Oh Chanukkah

This happy song is often sung in Yiddish. Hence, both the English and Yiddish versions are below. However, those who know Yiddish will quickly see that the English and Yiddish do not exactly correspond to each other. Both versions emphasize the secular aspects of Hanukkah, yet have a little reference to the religious aspect of the holiday. For the best rendition of this popular song, purchase *Oy Hanukkah*, a CD produced by the Klezmer Conservatory Band.

English Version
Chanukkah, Oh Chanukkah
Come light the menorah!
Let's have a party
We'll all dance the hora.
Gather round the table, we'll have a treat.
Shiny tops to play with, latkes to eat.

And while we are playing,
The candles are burning low.
One for each night, they shed a sweet light
To remind us of days long ago.

Yiddish Version
Chanukkah, O Chanukkah, a yontev a sheyner!
A lustiger a freylicher, nito noch azoyner.
Ale nacht in dreydl shpiln mir.
Zudigheyse latkes esn mir, geshvinder tsindt kinder,
Di dininke lichtelech on.
Zogt "al ha-nisim," loybt Got far di nisim
Un kumt gicher tantsn in kon

Arts and Crafts

1. How to Make Hanukkiot

A Clay Hanukkiah
Roll soft clay into a rope approximately ¾ inches thick. Punch holes evenly spaced across the base of the hanukkiah with a pencil or other round instrument, such as a Hanukkah candle. Allow the clay to harden a bit and then scratch letters or a design with a nail or toothpick. After the hanukkiah is completely dry, it may be painted with poster paints or enamel. If poster paints are used, cover it with a coat of shellac after the paint is dry.

A Potato Hanukkiah
Cut four potatoes in half. Place the flat sides down and bore a hole in the top of each half to hold the candles. For the shamash, use a whole potato cutting off about ¼ inch giving it a

flat surface; bore a hole in the top for the candle. Line the holes with aluminum foil. The potato hanukkiah can be arranged on a board or tray. Apples may be used instead of potatoes.

An Oil Hanukkiah
Fill nine wine cups with olive oil. Place a floating wick in each cup. Line up the cups in a line on a shelf, table, board, etc. Refill the cups with olive oil as it is used throughout the week.

2. Children's Colour Pages
Use the illustrations at the end of this chapter for children's colouring pages. Enlarge the graphics to fit standard size paper. Make as many copies of each as you have children who will want to colour.

Hanukkah Food
Many of the special dishes served during this festive season are cooked in oil.

1. Potato Latkes
This one has more vegetables for a heartier meal should you prefer it.

4 potatoes, peeled and shredded
2 carrots peeled and shredded
1 zucchini, shredded
1 large onion, chopped
2 tbsp. lemon juice
4 eggs
3 tbsp. flour
1 tsp. salt

Directions:
After the potatoes are shredded, immediately coat them in the lemon juice. After that, add the rest of the ingredients and mix well. In a large heavy skillet, heat about 1/8 inch oil. Using a spoon, spoon 1 large tablespoon full of batter into the oil

and flatten with the back of the spoon. Let it cook for about 3–5 minutes until it is golden brown, turning only once. Drain it on paper towels and serve immediately with the choices of sour cream, applesauce, or ketchup for your guests and/or family to choose from.

You can make sweet latkes by eliminating the above vegetables and substituting with sweet potatoes and 2 tbsp. honey or maple syrup. Top these delicious latkes with whipped cream and a dash of cinnamon! Enjoy.

2. Mini Sufganiyot

225 grams butter (8 oz. or 1 cup)
2 cups whole wheat (or preferred) flour
Pinch of salt
10 eggs

Directions:

Bring 1 cup of water to a boil in a large skillet and add the butter. Continue boiling until the butter is melted. Add the flour and salt and mix with a wooden spoon until the mixture forms a dough ball. Remove from flame.

Beat the eggs, 2 at a time, into the batter making sure that the previous ones where completely absorbed before adding more. In a large saucepan with heated oil, drop the dough in one teaspoon at a time. Allow the balls to puff, turning occasionally. Remove with a slotted spoon and drain on paper towels. Dip the balls into warmed honey, maple syrup or a mixture of cinnamon and sugar if you prefer. Or, do it Israeli style and fill your Sufganiyot with various jams or fruit pastes!

This recipe suggestion is a wonderful child's project. None the less, this is a tasty snack for both adult and child. Have Fun!

3. Edible Menorot

1 loaf of bread
1 jar of peanut butter

1 bag of short stick pretzels
1 bag of raisins (preferably golden)

Directions:
The children will love making this one. If you have several children present, set up a working table so they can all do this together. Spread out the supplies down the middle of a work space with the children able to line up on both sides of the table. Then each child can create their own masterpiece!

One slice at a time, evenly spread peanut butter on the bread. Following that, carefully lay down 9 pretzels vertically on the bread. Show the children how to leave space at the top of the pretzel sticks to add the raisin "flames" to the top of each stick.

One may add extra pretzels for a bottom if there is enough space, making it look like a menorah.

Place one raisin at the tip of each pretzel to represent the flame. Enjoy this snack as you watch the faces of your children glow like candles on the hanukkiah!

Appendix A
Dates for Hanukkah Celebration

2006	5767	16–24 December
2007	5768	5–13 December
2008	5769	22–30 December
2009	5770	12–20 December
2010	5771	2–10 December
2011	5772	21–29 December
2012	5773	9–17 December
2013	5774	28 November–5 December
2014	5775	17–25 December
2015	5776	7–15 December
2016	5777	25 December–1 January
2017	5778	13–21 December
2018	5779	3–11 December
2019	5780	23–31 December
2020	5781	11–19 December

Appendix B
Helpful Hanukkah Web sites

1. Music

www.tiwestport.org/chanukah/songs.html
Songs with words and sheet music

www.zemerl.com/cgibin/display.pl?subcategory=Hannukkah
A marvelous site—has about 40 songs! They usually come with translation, some with recording some with history.

www.theholidayspot.com/hanukkah/music
music downloads

www.songsforteaching.com/hanukkah
Another great site with everything

2. Recipes

www.pastrywiz.com/archive/category/hanukkah
This site includes loads of recipes for other holidays.

www.cyberkitchen.com/rfcj/category.cgi?category=HANUKKA
Here you can find more latkes recipes than you'll ever eat—great site!

3. Hanukkah Cards

www.holidays.net/chanukah

4. Children and Educational Emphasis

BILLY BEAR'S HANUKKAH
www.billybear4kids.com/holidays/hanukkah/hanukkah

TORAH TOTS
www.torahtots.com/holidays/chanuka/chanuk
Includes series of stories, educational materials, etc.

KIDS DOMAIN
www.kidsdomain.com/holiday/chanukah/index
Offers online games, word puzzles, printable colouring

EDUCATION WORLD ® LESSON PLANNING: A WORLD OF LEARNING HANUKKAH
www.education-world.com/a_lesson/lesson040

5. In General

JUDAISM 101: CHANUKKAH
www.jewfaq.org/holiday7
Discusses Hanukkah and its historical background. Includes the rules for playing dreidel and a recipe for latkes (potato pancakes).

6. Hanukkah Gifts, Menorah, Judaica

MESSIANICJEWISH.NET: MESSIANIC JEWISH WEBSTORE
www.messianicjewish.net/webstore.
The largest publisher and distributor of Messianic Jewish books, Judaica, gifts and other materials.

MESSIANIC JUDAICA WEBRING
www.v.webring.com/hub?ring=messianicjudaica
The Messianic Judaica Webring is an exciting new ring to bring together the world of Messianic Judaica to one place.

HANUKKAH DREIDELS, MENORAHS, CHANUKAH PLASTIC DREIDELS, CHOCOLATE GELT
www.chanuka.com
Learn about Hanukkah, light a menorah, and celebrate the festival of lights.

WESPREADTHEWORD.NET: MESSIANIC JUDAICA
www.wespreadtheword.net/Shopping/Messianic_Judaica

MESSIANIC JEWISH GIFTS
www.blow-the-shofar-in-zion.com

Scripture Index

The arrangement of the Biblical books below is the order found in the Hebrew Bible.

Bibliography

Arndt, William F. and Gingrich, F. Wilbur. *A Greek-English Lexicon of the New Testament and Other Early Christian Literature.* Chicago: The University of Chicago Press, 1957, 1973.

Birnbaum, Philip. *Daily Prayer Book: HaSiddur HaShalem.* New York: Hebrew Publishing Co., ND.

Bloch, Abraham P. *The Historical and Biblical Background of the Jewish Holy Days.* New York: KTAV Publishing House, 1978.

Bolen, Todd. *Pictorial Library of Bible Lands,* 4 CD's of original photographs, categorized and labelled. © 2000 by Todd Bolen. Now published by Kregel.

Brenton, Lancelot C.L. *The Septuagint with Apocrypha: Greek and English.* London: Samuel Bagster & Sons, Ltd., 1851. Reprinted by Hendrickson Publishers, Peabody, MA, 1992.

Brown, Colin, ed. *The Dictionary of New Testament Theology,* 3 vols. Grand Rapids: Zondervan, 1967, 1979.

Edelheit, Abraham J and Hershel. *History of the Holocaust: A Handbook and Dictionary.* Boulder, CO: Westview Press, 1994.

Goldstein, Jonathan, A. *1 Maccabees: A New Translation with Introduction and Commentary.* (Part of the *Anchor Bible*), Garden City, NY: Doubleday and Company, Inc., 1976, 1981.

Goodspeed, Edgar, J., trans. *The Apocrypha: An American Translation.* New York: Random House, reprint: the University of Chicago Press, 1939, 1958.

Goodman, Philip. *The Hanukkah Anthology.* Philadelphia: The Jewish Publication Society, 1992.

Josephus, Flavius. *Complete Works of Josephus.* (Translated by William Whiston. Grand Rapids: Kregel, 1978.

Pearlman, Moshe. *The Maccabees.* New York: Macmillan, 1974.

Scrocco, Jean L. ed. *Treasures of Hanukkah*. Parsippany, N. J.: The Unicorn Publishing House, Inc., 1987.

Strassfeld, Michael. *The Jewish Holidays: A Guide and Commentary*. New York: Harper and Row Publishers, 1985.

Trepp, Rabbi Leo. *The Complete Book of Jewish Observance*. New York: Behrman House, 1980.

Waskow, Arthur I. *Seasons of Our Joy*. New York: Summit Books, 1982.

The Eternal Light

A candle is a small thing.

But one candle can light another.

And see how its own light increases,
as a candle gives its flame to the other.

You are such a light.

Light is the power to dispel darkness.

You have this power to move back
the darkness in yourself and in others—
to do so with the birth of light
created when one mind illuminates another,
when one heart kindles another,
when one person strengthens another.

And its flame enlarges within you
as you pass it on.

Throughout history,
children of darkness have tried
to smother this passage of light
from man to man.

Throughout history, dictators large and small
have tried to darken, diminish
and separate men by force.

But always in the end they fail.

For always, somewhere in the world,
the light remains;
ready to burn its brightest
where it is dark;
a light that began
when God created the world.

And every free people has remained free
by resisting those who would
extinguish in men the light
of freedom,
of love,
of truth.

To do our daily part to increase this light,
we must remember that a candle alone is a small thing,
a man alone is a small thing,
a nation alone is a small thing.

Remembering this,
we must recognize something much more
than our indispensability to others.

We must also remember their indispensability to us.

We cannot hope –
either as individuals, or nations–
to reach our highest capabilities
until we help those around us reach theirs.

To be strong
the strong must serve.

"These lights we now kindle..."

These words accompany the lighting
of Hanukkah candles in the home,
and in the heart,
to commemorate the eternal bridge of light
which reaches from Creation itself
to the radiant spirit of free men.

In this spirit is celebrated
the Festival of Hanukkah–
the Festival of Light–
wherein the candle that gives its light
to the others is called
"the servant candle."

You too are strongest...
when you serve.

From "Birthday of the World"
By Moshe Davis and Victor Ratnor
Associated with the
Jewish Theological Seminary of America
when they wrote this

Printed with permission from the publisher:
Farrar, Straus and Giroux, LLC *Book Publishers*

Shoreshim Publishing
is the home of publication materials produced by

Torah
Resources
International
www.torahrediscovered.com

To contact the authors:
Ariel and D'vorah Berkowitz
torahrediscovered@mac.com
P.O. Box 31489
Jerusalem 91314 ISRAEL

Ariel and D'vorah are also the authors of the popular book, *Torah Rediscovered,* now published in German, Dutch, and Swedish.

Torah Rediscovered...

- has proven to be a tremendously helpful book to many people from many nations over the last 9 years.

- lovingly challenges readers, Jewish and non-Jewish alike, to take an honest new look at the true nature of the first five books of the Bible (the Torah).

- reveals the beauty and depth of God's divine covenantal revelation.

- attempts to demonstrate to all who seek to understand it how its divinely inspired pages can help them to learn in greater depth what it means to be new creations in Messiah.

Join hundreds of others from all around the world and order your copies of *Torah Rediscovered* today! Shoreshim Publishing, Inc is the only official publisher and distributor of Torah Rediscovered.

For information on other publications by these authors, please see the website of their publisher, **Shoreshim Publishing, Inc.** www.shoreshim.com